ALLEN CARR'S
Easy Way
to be
SUCCESSFUL

ALLEN CARR'S
Easy Way
to be
SUCCESSFUL

ARCTURUS

ALLEN CARR

Allen Carr wrote his best-selling Easy Way to Stop Smoking in 1985 after spending two years formulating his revolutionary method. Prior to his discovery of Easyway he had been addicted to nicotine and for a third of a century had chain-smoked between 60 and 100 cigarettes a day. Allen devised Easyway to help himself stop smoking but once convinced of its effectiveness he set about helping others. Encouraged by the phenomenal success of that first book, he started to build the network of clinics bearing his name that now spans the globe.

A full list of Allen Carr clinics appears at the back of this book. Should you require any assistance, do not hesitate to contact your nearest therapist.

Arcturus Publishing
26/27 Bickels Yard, 151–153 Bermondsey Street,
London SE1 3HA

Published in association with
foulsham
W. Foulsham & Co. Ltd
The Publishing House, Bennetts Close, Cippenham,
Slough, Berkshire, SL1 5AP, England

ISBN 0-572-02864-4

Printed and bound in India

INTRODUCTION

Initially I was very dubious about calling this book The Easy Way to Success. I cast my mind back to the years when I was struggling to clamber over the huge boulders that seemed to lie across my path, preventing contentment or satisfaction. I should have been very pleased with myself because I had acquired the outward trappings of success. Instead I was disappointed and unhappy. I stayed like that until I discovered the key to removing the obstacles that prevented me from being a success in my own eyes. I called that key Easyway.

As everyone's path in life is different so is each individual's definition and experience of success. I am quite keen on definitions, because they force us to be mindful of how we use language. Too often the scope of the word 'success' is limited to activities that bring fame and wealth. This book is about how to be successful on your own terms, and this means finding your own definition.

Serendipity or lucky accident has played a central role in what I deem to be my success. If you look at the life stories of other successful people, you will also find this element. Whether it was being in the right place at the right time or meeting the right person at the right time, serendipity had a hand in shaping their destiny. Webster's dictionary defines serendipity as 'the gift of finding valuable or agreeable things not sought for.'

In this book I want to show you how to maximize the chances of those valuable or agreeable happening to you. Once they do, you will discover the true meaning of success.

WHAT IS SUCCESS?

My dictionary states that it is 1. a favourable outcome, accomplishment of what was aimed at, attainment of wealth or fame or position; and 2. Thing or person that turns out well. That's quite a range and, of course, everyone reading this book will have a different idea of success. Can Easyway really make each one of them successful? I can only give them, and you, the key. I can't make them use it, any more than I could force you to eat a doughnut if you didn't want to. You have absolutely nothing to lose by reading this book, and the fact that you've bought it suggests that you think you lack success. But what sort of success are you after?

WHAT IS IT TO BE SUCCESSFUL?

The answer to this depends on what sort of person you are and what you value. Everybody wants to be successful, in that they want to feel their lives are worthwhile. People validate themselves in very different ways, but usually this validation requires some external manifestation or visible proof of success. Our concepts of success are invariably not of our own making, and are initially learnt from parents or friends. As we grow into adulthood we become aware that the first part of the definition given for success is the one to which most people subscribe, especially the bit about the 'attainment of wealth or fame or position'.

BRANDING SUCCESS

Given the media's preoccupation with wealth, fame and beauty, you could be forgiven for believing that success depends on one of those attributes. People who have all three are perceived as being even more successful and desirable and thus are placed even further above the rest of us. Articles and programmes devoted to lifestyle are selling us a particular brand of success. But it is only one brand. Unfortunately, when it comes to success, people are too willing to buy into the one that is being heavily promoted. If that is the kind of success you want to achieve, the last thing you should do is buy into it, because you are starting from a position of disadvantage.

THE BRAINWASHING/1

You believe you are unsuccessful because your life doesn't match or mirror some notional ideal that you have been told – and you accept – is what constitutes success. You want the big house, the adoring crowds, the glamorous parties, the expensive cars, the designer clothes, the media attention. Ask yourself how you are being successful by experiencing any of these things. These are merely by-products of some sorts of success, but by no means all. Wearing an expensive designer suit, driving a car that attracts envious glances or bathing in some exotic gel that's triple the price of most others on the drug store shelf won't make you any different. You are still you. There is a world of difference between living out the fantasy of success and actually being a success.

THE BRAINWASHING/2

We've been brainwashed to believe that splashing out on that expensive dress or car will make us feel just the ticket about ourselves, just as we've been duped into thinking that smoking a superior brand of cigarette or drinking a bottle of recommended vintage wine will mark us out as special. The positive effects we think they are going to give us usually don't last very long. The buzz we get from wearing the dress or driving the car quickly diminishes, and with physical addictions like alcohol and nicotine a top-up is needed almost as soon as the cigarette is stubbed out or the glass drained. None of these objects changes our situation one iota, and by buying them we are just financing an illusion of some ad man's devising. The only people we're making successful are the makers and their agents

THE FANTASY FACTOR

Unfortunately trying to live the fantasy of being a success can actually endanger our chances of becoming successful. You have only to read about the number of people crippled by debt because they wanted to acquire the must-have items they were told they needed to be truly happy to realize that consuming to be successful is a trap. In any transaction it is important that we come away from it with our integrity intact. Spending beyond our means actually undermines our integrity because we are engaging in a lie with ourselves. If you are constantly trying to cope with the worry of debt your mind will not be free to concentrate on positive activities that will make you truly successful.

MONEY AS SUCCESS

Most men and women who have made a lot of money by their own efforts aren't avid consumers. Indeed many of them are pretty tight when it comes to spending money. Their goal wasn't to become successful in order to spend wildly or appear glamorous or be invited on to chat shows. They became successful because they had a talent for something which they pursued to the best of their ability.

LIFTING THE VEIL

The trappings of success often conceal a fragile ego. To be successful you have to be highly motivated, and if you look into the backgrounds of a lot of famous or self-made people you will find them marked by unhappiness and deprivation. In fact, I have a theory that the slippery pole is more difficult to climb for people from loving, well-adjusted families, because in the main those folk are not as ruthless or uncaring. They are also probably more easily satisfied with 'small' successes, such as a happy home life. The person with an emotional history characterized by rejection or indifference would regard that as unachievable but probably be a whizz at master-minding a multi-million dollar take-over bid or directing a Hollywood block-buster.

RECIPE FOR SUCCESS

If the trappings of success are what you crave then the recipe is very straightforward. You find an occupation with fame or money-making potential and you put your all into getting to the top and don't mind about the casualties you incur en route. That's not the Easyway, though. The success I want to share with you is holistic. This means that the Easyway key won't work for those motivated by greed or self-aggrandizement alone.

THE MEANS

We know in our heart of hearts that having a lot of money is not a definition of success. If that were the case we would be validating the lives of some very dubious characters indeed. There are villainous, ruthless people who have acquired all the trappings of respectability but who do not deserve our respect or admiration. The means by which we acquire success do matter. To be worthwhile success must not be gained at the expense of others or be to their detriment. It must harm no one.

THE APPEARANCE OF SUCCESS

If you're going to take financial remuneration earned honestly as your measure of success, then I used to be one of those successful people. OK, I wasn't on football-player level but by most people's standards I was doing very nicely, thank you. However, I didn't regard myself as a success. The job paid well and gave me professional status, but I hated it. Smoking and heavy drinking went with the lifestyle – in those days it was chic to smoke, and successful professional men were expected to drink hard spirits. Beer was for 'working' men. Social brainwashing was just as prevalent then, only less obvious and so in some ways more insidious. I looked the part of successful man but inside I was weighed down by the burden of failure.

IGNORANCE

Smoking is just one of the countless burdens that we allow to sap us and prevent us from leading successful lives. We need to see them for what they really are. It is very easy to have a distorted view of them, especially if we have believed the brainwashing that they equate with glamour or success. For years I thought that cigarettes were my best friend. They were always there when I needed them. The reality, of course, was that I made them indispensable. They didn't really cheer me up, see me through black moods or enable me to cope better with life's tragedies or irritations. I just applied a winning persona to them because the nicotine made me crave their company. Such burdens become obstacles to success, but we are blind to their effect. An inability or unwillingness to see aspects of our lives as they truly are can have a stultifying effect on our development as people.

THE BURDEN

Once I saw through the deception of nicotine and escaped from the trap, I released myself in many other ways, too. Easyway revolutionized my life. You might think I'm bound to surround my transformation from smoker to non-smoker with a rosy glow. But don't just take my word for it. I could show you thousands of letters from men and women who have stopped smoking thanks to my method and in those letters they describe exactly the same sort of elation that I experienced. Smoking was a major millstone in my life, as it was in theirs. It dragged me down, and made my world seem dull, grey and worthless until the discovery of Easyway helped me to throw it off.

DISCARDING THE MILLSTONE

Take a long hard look at the things you think you depend on. Even minor superstitions – such as never answering the telephone until it has rung so many times or insisting on drinking out of a certain mug – can be tell-tale signs that we are losing faith in ourselves. Yes, I know, you can name any number of tycoons who have very peculiar predilections, so how can such foibles hinder success? Because the Easyway definition of success isn't based on someone's ability to make mounds of money, become a household name or reach the top of their chosen profession. Each and every one of us can be a success. It is up to us to choose our terms.

YOUR CHOICE

So what are your terms? These will probably depend on many different factors. The one thing you will have in common with everyone else who reads this book is dissatisfaction with where you are right now. I won't pretend that I can provide you with some short cut guide to fame, riches, true love, the perfect body or job, a panacea for all your perceived ills. I would be some sort of genius if I could do that, and I'm not sure that I would want to do it anyway. One of the many joys in life is discovering the true meaning of things for ourselves. There's nothing worse than someone telling you what you should be doing with yourself or your life. I want you to choose the kind of success you want. But first I want you to keep an open mind.

KEEPING AN OPEN MIND

I urge all my clients to do this, regardless of the problem they come to me with. I want you to get a great deal out of this book, and obviously I hope that what I share with you will sound a chord. Easyway is really very simple. It works because it is irrefutable, but it relies on you to test it and be certain of it. I want you to know that what I say is true, because you have thought about the ideas I present. The success you seek, in whatever area, will depend on you keeping an open mind. Foolish people are never successful. They might appear so, but appearances and truth are very different. Don't accept an idea unless it passes your truth test.

POTENTIAL

When we are young we are perhaps most aware of our potential. We believe in our immortality and that everything is possible. Of course, until we try and have lived a little we don't know where the limits of our potential are, either those we impose on ourselves or those laid down by others. Youth dares to take risks, whereas with age we tend to turn away from challenges to which we fear we may be unequal. If by middle age we have not achieved what constitutes our definition of success, this does not mean we have gone beyond any opportunity of achieving it. If the desire and conviction are still there so are the means.

DECIDING YOUR OWN FUTURE

Decision-paralysis is said to be very common among the young, and perhaps surprisingly especially among those who have received the benefits of higher education. Many young graduates have become so used to having their future mapped out for them – by the combined forces of their parents and the education system – that they are unprepared for dealing with the real world when they enter it. In order to make the right choices for ourselves we must be used to making decisions and not be reliant on other people making them for us, no matter how well meaning.

CLEVER CLOGS

Intellectual cleverness is widely admired, and yet it is interesting how little use it is as a measure of real achievement. Some of the greatest figures in world history were not considered that bright by their contemporaries. Albert Einstein was an employee of the Swiss Patent Office when he wrote his paper on the theory of special relativity, after his studies at the polytechnic in Zurich had not encouraged the authorities to invite him to undertake post-graduate research there. Winston Churchill was considered too dense to study classics, and so had more English lessons than many of his fellows. Despite the contempt of his tutors, he became a great orator with a superb command of English and as a character developed a steely resolution that would equip him for his greatest public role as a war leader. Charles Darwin failed to uphold the family tradition in the medical profession and then flirted with the idea of becoming a clergyman before finding his true path as a naturalist. He was never an academic, though, and when he wrote 'The Origin of Species' he was a country gentleman. Never be intimidated by academic achievement or dismissive of those who lack it.

COMMON SENSE

Practical skills are as valuable as academic ones. IQ tests are merely measures of brightness. They tell us nothing of a person's ability to think creatively, to interrelate with others, to get a job done. Success in life is often more dependent on inter-personal skills and sheer likeability than academic brilliance. In some instances a pronounced sense of our own cleverness can actually prevent us from reaching our potential. If we have gone through life being told how special we are because we are bright, there can be a tendency to expect success to fall into our lap. An appetite for hard work and a practical approach to achieving our desires is more likely to bring us success than a too well-developed sense of intellectual superiority.

THE ILLUSIONS OF SUCCESS

We live in an age that tells us that fame and success are mutually dependent – ie, you can't have the one without the other. This is to horribly distort the true state of affairs. Unfortunately, many young people buy into this illusion. They are desperate to be famous, because they think it is the ultimate in existence – life just doesn't get any better. What many of them overlook is that in order for this existence to have any validity the famous person has to be famous for doing something.

END GAMING

Wanting success for its own sake is the ultimate in end gaming. It's a bit like taking a train ride through breath-takingly beautiful scenery but not noticing any of it because your eyes and thoughts are focused on your destination. The problem with end-gaming is that you miss out on absorbing lessons and understanding that would stand you in good stead when you do reach that destination. It is possible to achieve a goal without being the better for it. The question is whether you would then be able to capitalize on that initial success without at some point filling the gaps in your understanding. It is never too late, of course, to apply your energies to some task that has meaning beyond the material reward it promises.

FINDING A PURPOSE

Finding a purpose in life can be hellishly difficult, especially if we have been brainwashed into believing that only certain types of 'doing' are worthwhile. If you think like this, you've probably discounted the idea that you could ever be a success. Not true. Let's forget the one-in-a-hundred million types of success and look at your needs as an individual. Sometimes we don't appreciate their nature until we have tried and failed, possibly several times. My only reason for becoming a chartered accountant was that the careers master told me that I was good at maths and he recommended that I should study accountancy. I had no idea what it involved. I found out and eventually had to admit to myself that I hated it. Then I moved on. If you weren't in your present job, what would you like to be doing?

WHAT DO YOU WANT OUT OF LIFE?

If you are to be successful, you have to know what you want, in terms of what is important to you. For many of us this is very difficult. You might see a garment you like the look of through a shop window but once you have it in your hands, or indeed try it on you, you find it fits in all the wrong places. What we think we want in theory often does not suit us in reality. Usually finding what we want is a process of elimination. What we want will probably change. Believing that we want something, even if that something is the wrong thing, gives us direction. We may not end up either wanting or achieving that initial objective, but just having it enables us to achieve something else worthwhile.

UNDERSTANDING OUR PURPOSE

A purpose is vital if we are to think anything of ourselves. Often we don't understand what this can be and suffer as a consequence. Depression, anxiety, tiredness, even physical illness can be caused by lack of direction and drift. Even highly motivated people sometimes disappear into these states when things aren't going well and they're disappointed with themselves. But they never lose sight of their goal or let it put them off for very long. If there is something you really want to do, don't talk or think yourself down. You'll face enough obstacles to making it reality without contributing to them.

INFERIORITY COMPLEXES

High social status confers many advantages, which is why so many people are keen to achieve it. Quite apart from the purely financial benefits that go with being one of life's 'winners', there is a psychological feel-good factor, too. At the other end of the scale, the so-called 'losers' are badly affected by how they perceive themselves and how they think others perceive them. The negative feelings raised by these perceptions put the body under constant stress and are responsible for higher rates of degenerative disorders such as cancer and heart disease. Even people in white-collar professions where some grading system is in operation are susceptible to the negative mind-set that arises out of inequality. If we are to achieve all-round success, we have to find ourselves a rung in the comfort zone of the social ladder or be strong enough to withstand society's negative value judgements. Always think of yourself as the equal of others, even if your financial means are slender and your status relatively lowly.

THE LOTTERY OF LIFE

What a cliché! And if you believe it, you must think you're part of it. We can make life a lottery by behaving as though it were. But you have as much control over it as you want to exercise. OK, so you can't single-handedly stop wars, change the minds of politicians or right the world's many wrongs. You do, though, have a great deal of say in how you live your life: what you say to other people, how you treat them, the decisions you take. In many ways your behaviour can make a difference to your own life and the lives of the people whom your actions touch. You have power.

THE ENDS

The last statement might seem a bit unrealistic. You might argue that there will always be winners and losers in life: people who are prepared to strive and make sacrifices, take risks in order to achieve a certain result, against those who are not. That's perfectly true, but that doesn't mean we are at liberty to unfairly take advantage of others or behave as we please because we have formed the opinion that having a goal somehow makes us better and elevates our needs and desires.

WILLPOWER

Some people make a great deal out of willpower and believe you can achieve anything so long as you have it. I don't buy this. You can't will your way to success any more than you can will your way to give up smoking. The trouble with willpower methods is that they always leave you feeling short changed. If you don't want to do something for its own sake, you're not really committed and it's unlikely you'll be able to stick at it. We can push ourselves to achieve, certainly, but this only works in the short term. The idea of Easyway is not to give you intermittent success but to enable you to experience success as a constant in your life.

SELF-BELIEF

An essential quality of all successful people is sheer stickability. If you want success you have to keep going even when people around you may be casting doubt on your ability to get there. This is not to advise you to be so stubborn that you pay no attention to what others say, but to be sound in your judgements as to whose advice you do value. An essential quality of all successful people is their willingness to take responsibility for their decision-making. They believe in their ability to think through problems and come up with the right answer in any given set of circumstances. This is because they have never ducked the challenge of risking getting it wrong and making a mistake.

EXERCISING YOUR POWER

Follow your enthusiasms, if you recognize them. Loving what we do makes such a difference to how we live our lives. Of course, not everyone can make a hobby into a profession or way of earning a living. But you are much more likely to have a rewarding life if you can bring a natural enthusiasm to what you do. There is nothing more soul-destroying than hating what you spend 70 per cent of your waking time doing. The expression, 'Get a life!' was made for such people. My life didn't truly begin until I discovered Easyway.

DREAMS PAST

When I was young measures of success were firmly rooted in reality. At the time I was becoming aware of my environment and my place in it, the world was just beginning to lick the wounds it had sustained in the Second World War. Opportunities were not as plentiful or varied as they are now. There was also a great sense of people knowing their 'place' in society. If you got ideas above your station, you were soon slapped down, especially by your peers. Job aspirations didn't extend much further than boys wanting to get into white-collar employment, and girls following them as secretaries. We might've dreamt of owning a Rolls-Royce or a mink coat but it was only a dream. Reality was where you lived.

DREAMS PRESENT

People's expectations are much less modest, and ideas of success more grandiose than they used to be. Success is intrinsically linked to material prosperity and the glamorous lifestyle it can buy. When boys and girls are old enough to choose a career it is the bread-and-butter (ie, boring) occupations – plumbing, electrical engineering, surveying, for example – that are losing out to media studies and the like. The reason for this shift towards jobs in the service sector is not just that we are consuming more and so more opportunities are occurring in these industries. The perception of what constitutes a worthwhile job has changed.

MEASURING SUCCESS/1

If we're to believe what we're told by those people who like to think they're wired to modern consciousness and so can actually reflect what's going on in real life, men and women measure success in different ways. For men their perception of success is very closely bound up with how they are seen in relation to their peers. Being higher than other men in the social scale is all-important – and that means having a bigger car, better job, nicer house, more money. Further confirmation of superiority comes in the form of a pretty wife and bright children. For most men success is seen purely in material terms, measurable, quantifiable and eminently marketable.

MEASURING SUCCESS/2

There are of course women who see success in male terms – good career, fat pay-packet, etc. But women being the superior sex, their view is generally more complex, and encompasses wider needs. Women have had to devise methods of ensuring that they get what they want from life while attempting to minimize the cost to those who are dearest to them. While a man will focus on one thing and concentrate on that, a woman is able to take on and accomplish several tasks simultaneously. There is a lesson here for men: if there are people you care about, develop the skill of multi-tasking to ensure that any material or intellectual goal you set is not achieved at a painfully high price.

CHANGED PERCEPTIONS

No one, it seems, wants to do anything perceived as ordinary. And the people in these jobs have to be made to feel they are not as bad as everyone else thinks they are, so dustmen have been re-styled as Environmental Services Operatives, and people who used to be known collectively as clerks are now known as advisors or executives. Hardly jobs that are going to provide a passport to success, you might scoff. Perhaps not, but even a dustman can make a success of what he does. Remember: it's not what you do but how you do it that is the surest measure of self-worth and, ultimately, success.

HOW DO YOU DO?

It was the psychologist Carl Jung who said, 'Never ask a man what he does but how he does it.' To me this gets to the heart of the notion of measuring people in terms of their occupation. How many times have you been at a party or social gathering and someone you don't know has introduced themselves and then almost immediately asked, 'What do you do?'. It's one of those social conventions, I suppose, but it's also a dead giveaway. Whether that person is aware of it or not, they are sizing you up socially and materially. We are such competitive animals that the measuring stick is usually at the ready. It's the attitude of 'Never mind the quality of the person, note the height of their social standing'. I take exception to being assessed purely on the basis of who I am thought to be.

SERENDIPITY

I am a great believer in the role of chance – or serendipity – in our lives. I have had many occasions to thank chance for its efforts on my behalf. Some people explain it as some form of divine intervention. I don't know about that, but whatever its provenance I'm grateful to it. It is only because of serendipity that the most recent 20 years of my life have been so happy and fulfilling. The discovery of Easyway was almost entirely serendipitous or accidental. The only aspect of it that I can take credit for is being able to see how it could be exploited to benefit others. I suppose in that sense I was open to the possibilities that serendipity throws our way. This is important. Serendipity can't help us unless we create the conditions that allow it to occur.

WORK

Hard work has always been held up as being good for individuals, but work for its own sake isn't going to make a success of your life. Work has to be perceived as worthwhile by the person doing it if it is to have any value beyond the remuneration received for it. Some types of work are regarded as being better than others. Generally, of course, highly paid jobs are more coveted than less well paid occupations, although the latter may be far more beneficial to the wider society than the former; compare, for example, a stock broker with a nurse. Assess the value that you place on the work you do. If it has no value beyond your pay cheque, look for something worthwhile to put your efforts into.

FREE WILL

We are told that what differentiates us from animals is free will. Our mental and physical makeup may be to a certain extent predisposed, but that is only part of the story. Largely, we are free to choose a course of action or mode of behaviour over another. Some people who regard themselves as unsuccessful build an argument for why they can never be anything else. We have all been in situations where nothing seems to go right, but it would be a mistake to extrapolate from this that we are the hapless victims of circumstance. If things are continually going wrong for you, look at the decisions you are making. Don't blame life.

RESTING FROM THE GRINDSTONE

Our politicians contribute in no small measure to our paranoia about success. They make speeches exhorting us to produce more goods, to create more wealth, to give our all to what they call the enterprise economy. It's understandable, I suppose; they've got to keep money rolling into the public coffers and that money can only come from us taxpayers, and so they keep our noses to the grindstone of work. It would be no good to them if we all decided to become hermits or holy men content to live on crusts, nor do they care whether we are content with what we do for a living. But we must be aware for ourselves that there is more to life than simply earning. Paying attention to those other aspects makes us more productive as citizens not less.

STACKING THE ODDS

Conventional wisdom says that death and taxes are the only two certainties in life. Both arrive whether we want them or not. Success we almost certainly do want but is often regarded as one of those imponderables. The least worthy seem to get it in spades, at the expense of the most deserving. I don't believe that, and neither should you. Ask yourself why you are prepared to believe a generalization instead of trusting your ability to be successful. Your answer could be that the longer the odds are the less shame when you fail. People who want success work ceaselessly towards shortening those odds because they know that over time lengthening them only serves to make life more difficult. Find ways of shortening those odds.

YARDSTICKS

If we don't think we are successful, how can we be? I knew I wasn't a success because I hated myself for being prey to what I perceived as a major weakness – an inability to kick the habit of smoking. That was my yardstick, and I kept falling short of it. My particular difficulty was made worse by the fact that I had fallen into a trap that had been gaping open in front of me for years. When you have seen your father die of lung cancer you can't be innocent of the dangers of smoking or the prospects for the heavy smoker. Still I fell. My yardstick was self-made. I wasn't trying to live up to some notional ideal. Either way the principle is the same. The remedy is not, however. Look at your life and ask yourself what it would take for you to consider yourself a success.

GUILT

Quite often we take out our disappointment at not being who or what we want to be by blaming ourselves. There's a lot of guilt attached to being ordinary these days. Some people admit to feeling guilty because they are not doing something spectacular with their lives. The guilt usually only arises when they see someone pushing themselves to extremes in pursuit of a goal. If you are largely content with how your life is shaping up, it would be misguided to let a comparison make you feel bad about yourself. Let the person who wants to do something extraordinary get on with it. Wish them good luck, but don't castigate yourself with their apparent success. If you were to be aware of the minutiae of their lives, you'd probably discover that you were more successful in other ways.

THE WELL PROPORTIONED LIFE

Although it is important to have a healthy ego and a robust sense of our worth, we need also to be realistic about our capabilities. If our expectations – of a job, a relationship, even of ourselves – are insupportably high, we are doomed to disappointment. It is better to have something that is good enough – in that it satisfies some of our requirements – than to end up with nothing because we are not prepared to lower our sights. This is not to say that you shouldn't aim high initially but don't let pride leave you out uncomfortably on a limb. Don't try to fight life too long or hard. Sometimes it knows better than we do.

INDIVIDUAL STYLE

Have you noticed how many forms of social fascism we face nowadays? We're not even allowed to wear the clothes we want without some style guru telling us that we're letting ourselves down and projecting an image that will ensure we remain stuck in a rut. Only a certain appearance maketh the person, it would seem. Call me old-fashioned but I humbly beg to differ. I'm not condoning being badly dressed in the sense of looking scruffy or unkempt, but what an individual chooses to wear is really up to them. It may be that some people have to look a certain way to get on in their jobs. If those people are happy doing that and it doesn't cost them personally, fine. Perhaps they feel more comfortable conforming than questioning the purpose of fitting people into style camps.

FOLLOWING THE LEADERS

Even such a simple scenario as accepting the status quo raises questions about the sort of success we can expect from life. The people who don't give a damn for convention and are prepared to go their own way are life's natural leaders. It's unlikely that they will turn around to see if anyone else is following – that isn't the point. It is important to them to live life on their own terms. They would regard their inability to do this as failure.

THE BIG QUESTION

Why do you want to be successful? You're probably thinking what a daft question this is. Who doesn't want to be successful and be able to enjoy the good things in life? By the 'good things in life' I assume you would mean enjoying the benefits of more money. Apart from being a very narrow definition of success, this also reeks of wishful thinking. Success doesn't usually arrive on a wing and a prayer. To achieve success you have to have a purpose. Your purpose could be to make more money than you are earning now. You might have something in mind for which you want to use that money, perhaps a bigger house, a better car, to educate your children, to afford more or better holidays. Once a certain level of material success is achieved the initial purpose for wanting money is no longer valid.

CONTROL FREAKERY

All of us like to feel we are in control. It can be very unsettling when we find we are not and that despite our best efforts our plans are being turned upside down. Some people are so afraid of the prospect of not having control that they try to fix outcomes in advance. They are control freaks. This is not to say that you should not be organized or methodical in what you do, or not try to bring about a particular outcome that you believe is right. Control freaks are fearful that if they don't get their way they will be disadvantaged. They can't bear the thought of coming out of something second best. When events take on a life of their own and go beyond our control, sometimes the wisest course of action is to sit back and do nothing. The eventual outcome is always instructive. Control freaks don't trust life or themselves.

YOUR LIFE

It is very easy to fall into the trap of thinking that our lives are futile, that we don't matter as individuals, and that we are just making up the numbers. We might identify politicians, scientists, inventors, speculators or financiers as the real movers and shakers and decision-makers who are shaping our destiny. We are the insignificant 'us', whereas they are the great 'them'.

BACKING OUT

If you find yourself in a cul-de-sac, try a bit of lateral thinking. A common response when things go wrong is to look for somebody or something to blame. It might be another person, a particular circumstance or ourselves. When something negative happens it is not helpful to use up valuable emotional and mental energy compounding the negativity. Inflicting damage for a wrong done to us is never an appropriate response. If you are in a bad situation there is a limited range of positive actions available to you. Ask yourself the following questions: Can you alter the situation in some way? Can you walk away from it? Can you change yourself? Can you live with the situation? Your means of extricating yourself from the bad situation has to be one of these options. When you weigh up which of them is the right one, consider the effect your decision will have on other people as well as on yourself. You may well find yourself choosing between least worst options. In these circumstances the scope for a successful outcome is inevitably limited in the short term.

BEWARE OF SCAMS

Recently I received an unsolicited email from a company proclaiming that it could 'remove the obstacles that cause adults to lose hope'. They were offering – at a price, no doubt – to give me a degree, even a doctorate, to enable me to 'take part in the wealth' that is given automatically to employees with 'ZERO skills or experience, just because they have that piece of paper'. I was informed that the college and university transcripts handed out by this organization met the highest academic standards and that degrees were issued on premium diploma paper, bearing an official gold raised college seal.

I am a great believer in the benefits awarded us by the university of life, but this seemed a pretty tacky way of getting them. There will always be people who try to convince us – or con us – into thinking that there are valid short-cuts to obtaining our goals. There aren't.

TIME PASSES

But what if you've reached those middle years and success seems as far away as ever? That's as may be but it's not going to come any closer more quickly if you fall into the trap of clutching at straws. There are so many ways these days of obtaining qualifications through learning, for example, if that is what you feel is holding you back. When we leave something very late, and chastise ourselves for doing so, we should perhaps ask if that something is what we really want. Sometimes we hold a goal ahead of us without ever truly believing we can attain it. If we're not careful this can become a source of disappointment. Don't allow this to happen. Either re-double your efforts to achieve your goal or put it aside and admit it isn't the right one for you.

THE SCENIC ROUTE

We can become so confused by questions of what is our true path in life that we end up going the wrong way just because everything else is heading in that direction. It can seem so cut and dried – and yes, easy – for those who know exactly what they want. Often, though, the people who are sure they know what they want find it's not what they thought it was once they get up close and start examining their prize. There is a lot to be said for taking the longer scenic route. Your eyes have to be open all the time because you are really not sure where you are going and as a result you tend to absorb the lessons you learn. This is not always the case when we are sure of our route.

PARTNERING SUCCESS

I owe a tremendous debt of gratitude to my wife, Joyce, for her support through the years. Without her, I doubt that I would have achieved success with Easyway. You can't just pluck the ideal partner out of thin air, and having that partner won't necessarily ensure that you achieve all your goals. However, there is nothing like having a stable base from which to launch yourself at an unsuspecting world. You may come back down to earth with a bump several times – as I did in the early days – but having someone who believes in you and is prepared to challenge your thinking when necessary will ensure that you keep focused and that you have the confidence to keep trying.

CONCENTRATION

Trying to become successful can be a lonely business. Whether our goal is to launch a business, an idea, an actual product or a career, it takes a lot of time and energy. Even when we are not actively engaged in doing those hundreds of things towards making it a reality, we can feel its presence. It won't leave us alone, and in many ways we don't want it to. However hard it might seem, it is a good idea to allow yourself some respite. When we become too close to something we can lose sight of the overall picture and be disadvantaged by it. Allow yourself distractions. If you are engaged in work that takes a great deal of mental energy, counter-balance this with a regime of physical exercise. Remember to nourish both sides of your brain – the rational and the intuitive – and don't over-feed either.

ROLE MODELS

Some successful people can point to role models who inspired or influenced them positively and thus helped them to reach their goals. I didn't have a very encouraging start in this respect. Neither of my parents was inspiring or socially impressive. They made each other miserable and were incapable of meaningful communication with me or my brothers and sisters. But, despite the fact that we weren't on the same wavelength and they never guided me, I am convinced they prepared me for the life that lay ahead and in a strange way actually enabled me to get the most out of it. Just as we get the politicians we deserve, so perhaps do we also get the parents – or children – we deserve, or require for our particular development.

HERO WORSHIP

Undoubtedly we can use the example of others to spur ourselves on to achieve the success we want. Sometimes, though, we can be so in awe of the achievements of others that their example hobbles us instead of freeing us to go on to achieve on our own account. It is as though we have transferred our power to this other being, thereby short-changing ourselves. If our admiration for another person motivates us, that is good. But if it has the effect of making us feel bad about ourselves because we are convinced that person is better than us, then it is bad. We should never allow our admiration for others to be at the expense of our own self-esteem and self-belief.

NATURAL ABILITY

I was brought up to believe in natural ability, that you're either born with a particular talent or you're not. Look very hard at the people who tell you this. Often they have never tried to excel at anything, or perhaps they have tried and feel they failed in some way.

When I was a youngster I had no aptitude for boxing and certainly no liking of it, despite my hero-worship of the great heavyweight, Joe Louis. Practice born out of necessity – and the fear of getting a pasting – made me into more than a match for some very rough opposition. This experience taught me that ability can be honed out of very little. If you want to try something, don't think twice about whether or not you have natural ability. This will develop with practice and commitment.

HOLDING ON

When we are young, we believe that anything and everything is possible. We can see our name in lights. As we grow older the difficulties seem to mount up, burying our dreams. It can be a question of what might have been. We can come to regard this as natural, of reality overtaking us. We need to keep hold of that inner belief that burned in our younger selves if we are to realize our goals and achieve what we want.

ATTITUDES TO LIFE

How we regard life has a great bearing on what we get out of it, and this includes success. My mother believed that life on earth is to be endured and certainly not enjoyed. Unfortunately, she always expected difficulties and they obliged. It is said that depression lowers the body's immunity to disease. Weighed down by our sadness and negativity, it doesn't work as efficiently. Without a positive frame of mind we won't have a healthy body, and without a healthy body we won't be able to pursue our dreams.

PESSIMISM

Obviously it's not a good idea to bury our heads in the sand when things go wrong, but if we are chronically negative or pessimistic about everything, how can we raise ourselves to make the effort needed to put our energies into worthwhile projects? And even if we do our pessimism may well attract misfortune.

The pessimist will never experience success. Whatever they have or however much, they will never be satisfied. To be truly successful, we have to be able to recognize or acknowledge the pluses in our lives.

HUNCHES

Unless we are artists or engaged in creative work it is most likely that we use the right side of our brain more than the left. The right side of the brain is to do with rational thought, whereas the left side is to do with intuition or insight. Usually our decisions and actions are governed by reason, and for many people it is the best way – perhaps the only way – forward, even though the options chosen may not always be the best ones in the long run. Sometimes we may act only on a strong impulse or hunch, and get it absolutely right. Don't be afraid to act on your hunches. Try to give yourself enough 'quiet' time for them to occur to you.

PROBLEMS

When we encounter problems with what we are doing we try to think ourselves out of trouble. That is what our brains are for, after all. We should only follow this route so far, however. We've all been in the situation of laying awake at night for hours while we explore every inch of our problem, desperate for a solution and insistent that it must be in there if only we can tease it out. The best course of action in these circumstances is to switch off and go to sleep. If you let go you will find the solution comes to you. It might not be the next day or even the day after, but it will come.

BAD TIMES

The expression, 'These things are sent to try us' is a truism if ever there was one. The road to success might seem very smooth for some people, but that's probably because they make light of the bad times and see them as being inseparable from the whole adventure of achieving their goals. It's a fact about human beings that when life is going well for us we don't want to dwell on the times when it wasn't. Having a sense of proportion and not being afraid of facing adversity are vital characteristics if you are to be successful.

PARENTING/1

These days many parents feel that their main duty to their children is to ensure that they receive a good education and are equipped to pass the many exams they have to face with flying colours. Merely passing or scraping through is regarded as only one degree better than outright failure. You need top marks to get to the right university and gain admission to the right course. Competition is so fierce to push young people beyond their peers that parents are now actively engaged in the process, as sort of 'seconds' at the ringside of academic achievement. Mums and dads routinely ferry their charges to and from all kinds of activities which it is hoped will give them an advantage. There have always been parents who have taken an interest in their children's schooling, but now there seems to be anxiety attached to what should be a relatively trouble-free time in life. Parents are anxious because they're afraid their children won't succeed, and children are anxious because they are afraid of letting their parents down. Relax.

PARENTING/2

Every child needs to know that it is good at something in order to build confidence. However, unless being good at that something actually has meaning for the child it is unlikely to consider it worthwhile. I was very good at maths but it left me stone cold. Being good at something merely as a means to an end is a pretty empty proposition if someone is expected to base a great part of their life on it. Once a child is programmed by its parents to achieve it can be very difficult for that child to express its own wishes. It is up to parents to leave a space for the child to develop into. Filling every minute with some activity or purpose that you the parent have decided is beneficial can be damaging to a child's success in the long run. No child should be pressured to achieve beyond its ability, and every child should be allowed the freedom to discover what it wants to achieve for itself.

PARENTING/3

When we are desperate for our children to succeed in terms of securing a profitable job or career, and are prepared to go to great lengths to ensure this happens, we should examine our motives. It is quite common for parents to decide that their child should succeed where they perceive themselves to have failed. Perhaps the parent wanted to be a top-class singer, tennis player, lawyer or whatever and getting their child to succeed where they failed is a way of nullifying their own disappointment at that earlier failure. Quite apart from damaging the child, by in effect appropriating his or her life, they are also harming themselves. We cannot live fully through another person. Of course we can share experiences, good and bad, with others but each life takes its own direction and we cannot follow two tracks simultaneously.

LIVING IN THE SHADOWS

Although children, and especially teenagers, might give the opposite impression, most of them can be made sensitive to their place in the world. Living up to other people's expectations can be a great burden. The children of successful parents are often considered to have an easier path than those who are nonentities to the wider world – a string will be pulled and 'Hey, presto!' an advantageous opening will be found. The pressure, though, is always on to live up to the parent and perhaps even out-do them. Success in these terms is very narrowly predicated on appearances and measurable achievements. Once we are on this hook, it can be very difficult to take a wider view and consider the types of success we meet on a more personal level.

PROGRAMMING

You could be forgiven for thinking that with some people their path through life is pre-destined. Look at how many professions and trades seem to run in families. The type of life we settle into has a great deal to do with background and parental influence. But success is not about going through life on automatic pilot. The wife of a famous and greatly revered literary figure confessed at the end of her life to not having done anything that she really wanted to do. All her energies had gone into ensuring his success and reputation. When he died her purpose in life died with him and she spent her last twenty years in regret. Selflessness can bring its own success in the knowledge of a life well spent, but it must be genuine.

CAREERS GUIDANCE

When I was coming to the end of my schooling I attended a series of presentations by professionals who were trying to interest us in working in their particular line of business. I remember a local bank manager explaining how one in four of us could end up as managers and would earn a great deal of money. All but one of us was very impressed by this. When the manager said that banking gave insights into other professions, the one boy who was not impressed asked what were the chances of him becoming a groundsman. There was an outburst of laughter, as though he had cracked a joke. He was deadly earnest. He loved sport and he wanted to be a groundsman. I hope that boy went on to become one.

FRIENDS

Good friends are essential for our well being – and anything that is essential to that is essential to our success. Never be afraid to widen your circle of friends or to move away from one circle if an opportunity you want to pursue arises. True friends always remain with us no matter what. Physical distance, or lack of opportunity to meet regularly, are not friendship killers. Granted they make friendship more difficult, but they do not put paid to it. The friendships that last are the ones that don't need constant attention to keep them going. They are also the ones we don't deliberately cultivate but are spontaneous and natural.

THE COMPANY WE KEEP

Our progress through life can be greatly helped or hindered by the people we associate with, either through work or socially. Increasingly, though, our work colleagues are our friends, and in some cases the only ones we have. In some areas of employment, work now takes up so much time and energy that people aren't developing social lives away from the office. What little recreational time these people have is almost grafted onto the end of the working day, which is characterized by pressure, long hours and tight deadlines. What's wrong with that? Absolutely nothing if this free time is spent pleasantly unwinding and exchanging positive thoughts. But it is unlikely you will develop genuine friendships with colleagues if your time together is spent unproductively chewing over problems, back-biting about other colleagues and, in the case of the really insecure, bragging. For people with an ounce of sensitivity this scenario is psychologically harmful, and anyone who promotes it on a regular basis should be given a wide berth.

DECISION MAKING

Some decisions in life are taken for us, especially when we are young. I didn't have a burning desire to be a chartered accountant. In fact, I didn't have a burning desire to be anything. I was good at maths and the careers master advised me to go in that direction. We can only take decisions based on where we are in life and the experiences we have had to date. In the beginning we have very little to draw on. Although I'm not convinced that once we reach adulthood we are in sole charge of our destiny, we must try to take decisions that we know to be right for ourselves, based on the knowledge of ourselves that we have formed up to that point.

AMBITION

This is one of the main ingredients of success, some might say the key ingredient. Without ambition there is no doing, and how is it possible to be successful without a great deal of action? There is also another aspect to ambition, and that is the desire to 'be'. You can desire to be anything: a musician, a builder, thinner, taller, prettier, even just plain good. What you desire is your choice. The point is that if you want to 'be' you have to 'do' in order to bring it about.

THE ROAD TO SOMEWHERE

Sometimes we can feel as though we are marking time and not making any progress. This can be the case even when we have set a goal and we are doing our best to achieve it, but it's more pronounced when we're not sure where we are headed. I started my working career as an office boy in a firm of accountants. I was ambitious to get beyond licking stamps and making the tea, and eventually I did. The journey to becoming a chartered accountant was more rewarding than what happened subsequently, after I'd got my professional qualifications. Once I had arrived I discovered that I didn't want to be there. But I wouldn't have found this out unless I had been prepared to 'do' in the first instance. Life is full of cul-de-sacs, most of them instructive, and just as you found your way into them, you will find your way out. Discovering what isn't for us is as important as discovering what is.

SIZE MATTERS

Have you noticed how bigger is always portrayed as being better? In business terms it is always seen as the only way forward. Companies are encouraged to expand, to gobble up smaller operations or graft them onto their corporate body. If you are a businessman you are regarded as not fulfilling the potential of your business – ie, limiting its success – unless you want to grow it. In an article I read recently, many bosses of small companies were identified as being part of the 'problem' of staying small because they wanted to keep control of day-to-day management. The assumption was that the purpose of any business is to make as much money as possible and the only way of doing this is to expand. This seems to be a case of the tail wagging the dog. What of the purpose of the people involved in those businesses? If the well-being of the people who created them demands hands-on involvement, then expansion is clearly not for them. Never allow yourself to become a slave to theory.

REGRETS

We all make mistakes, and when we're pushing forward we are more liable to make them. When we make a bad decision it can knock our self-confidence and lead to a bout of self-recrimination. If this results in us looking objectively at ourselves and our motivation, all well and good. But merely chastising ourselves and regretting what we've done won't help us either to recover from it or to put matters right, if this is required. Dwelling on setbacks is a form of egotism, a bit of the 'poor me' syndrome. Dwell on the solution, and then only until you are satisfied you have found the right one.

PLEASING YOURSELF

Many people are deflected from following their own desires by a need to try to please others. It is said of politics that you can fool some of the people some of the time but you cannot fool all of the people all of the time. The same goes for pleasing them. The pleaser is invariably trying to get approval, love, attention or making up for some other perceived deficit. This is a recipe for unhappiness and frustration. By all means take other people into account in terms of how your actions might affect them, but don't allow your wishes and desires to be over-shadowed by theirs. Otherwise you will set up conflicts that will result in you pleasing no one, including yourself.

LETTING GO

All of us gather baggage as we go through life. By baggage I mean negative attachments that we become fixated on. We may not even realize we are in this situation. Everything just seems as normal. But it's a bit like deteriorating eyesight – the deterioration is so gradual often we do not realize it is happening until we find we can't see what normally sighted people can see. Our world is becoming smaller. Too great an attachment to certain ideas, people or possessions can have a similar effect. Success depends on us being clear sighted about ourselves, the people around us and the situations we find ourselves in. We have to accept the world as it is and not deceive ourselves that we know how it should be.

SELF-BELIEF

If we have belief in ourselves we have no need to fear other people, either their opinion or that they might be better than us. It took me a long time to work out that people would accept me at face value. If you present yourself in a certain way, people will accept that as the real you. Having self-belief means not accepting other people's opinions of us, especially the negative. What matters is to know who you are and to be comfortable with that being. Always hold fast to the old maxim: 'Sticks and stones may break my bones but names can never hurt me.'

CONFIDENCE

We can have this instilled in us from a very early age. As a young man I can remember feeling very gauche and unworldly when in the company of other young men who had been to public school and enjoyed the considerable benefits of their upbringing. None of them seemed to doubt for a moment that they would be leading men not following them and that they were destined for the top. Being with them didn't do much for my self-esteem, but nor did it make me want to be like them; not really, although at times I wished for their social graces. If your conscience is clear, you should never be ashamed to be what you are. The super-confidence that comes with expecting the world to shower you with its riches can blunt the appetite for life and genuine success.

EDUCATION VERSUS INTELLIGENCE

I used to believe that education and intelligence were the same thing, and greatly regretted the fact that I didn't go to university. I thought I wasn't bright enough, and my parents perpetuated this belief. It's far better to be intelligent than educated. You can use your intelligence to give yourself the education you lack, but education won't make you intelligent, no matter how many books you read or subjects you study. Our intelligence is one of our greatest assets. Develop it, harness it to help you achieve your goals.

BACKGROUND

We can be acutely aware of not belonging to the 'right' class or social group, but it would be a mistake to believe this can hold us back. I used to have a bit of a chip on my shoulder when it came to the Hooray Henrys I worked with. In time I became more aware of the similarities between us than the differences. Our upbringing coats us in a thin veneer which is easily scratched off. It is the person beneath this veneer that counts. Each of us has the ability to observe, learn and develop his character or skills – all the requisites necessary for success.

WISHFUL THINKING

Many of us drift through life, hoping something will turn up to give us a purpose. We look round at other people and are easily persuaded that they have got it made; the other (wo)man's grass is always greener when we are unsure of our own direction. That expression 'having it made' says a lot about how we regard success. Until we start examining the true state of affairs we can persuade ourselves that success comes ready-made for our consumption, like some commodity. Success has to be created by us. It isn't sitting out there waiting for our call.

ACKNOWLEDGE YOUR LIMITS

Undoubtedly success has to be worked for, and sometimes very hard indeed. We've all read stories of people working eighteen-hour days or perhaps working by day and studying by night in order to achieve a goal. Just as there are many different types of success, so there are different ways of acquiring it. Don't get me wrong, all of them require hard work and commitment, but they don't demand that you turn yourself into a nervous or physical wreck. Some people have a greater capacity for pushing themselves to the limit, although generally they can't keep this up indefinitely without it taking its toll. You must be aware of your limits. In order to find them you will probably have to exceed them at least once. When you know for sure where the boundary lies, try to work within it.

STIMULANTS

We can be persuaded to believe that a bit of chemical assistance will help to keep us in hot pursuit of our goal. We might not think twice about skipping breakfast and lunch but that cup of coffee or cigarette is never similarly forsaken. We might not make a conscious decision to increase our consumption, but up it goes. In fact by relying on such crutches we are making harder work of achieving success. All artificial stimulants come at a price, and it's your health that pays. They take far more out of you than they give back in short- term boosting. There's not much point achieving success and then finding you can't enjoy or prolong it because your body is exhausted.

YOUR BODY IS A TEMPLE

When we put unreasonable demands on the body we are in turn short-changed by it. My dependency on tobacco reduced me to a pitiable state, unable to enjoy life because I felt over-shadowed by the 'big monster'. Clearly not all smokers are prepared to examine or even acknowledge the down side of smoking, just as people who rely on junk food don't want to be told that they are poisoning their bodies rather than nourishing them. Why does this matter? Unless we are extraordinarily lucky, how we treat our body and what we put into it will affect our performance over time. We can get away with abusing ourselves when we are young because the body is incredibly resilient, but as we grow older the IOUs start rolling in. Success is hard enough to achieve without hobbling ourselves physically.

SUPER BEINGS

Our illusions about what it means to be a success can put us off trying to achieve it for ourselves. This is especially the case if we are inclined to accept the 'them and us' classification of humanity: 'them' denoting the people who have 'made it', and 'us' the vast majority who are standing and staring, with noses pressed against the glass divide. People who have achieved success aren't super beings with more and better faculties. See most successful people in the flesh and they look pretty ordinary. They are human beings who, by one means or another, have managed to harness their energy towards a particular end.

KEEPING YOUR DISTANCE

Never allow yourself to become so bound up with a project, situation or person that you are unable to stand back from time to time and take stock of it. If it is of genuine value, your appreciation will be all the greater, whereas if there are any negative aspects these will make themselves known to you. Most of us have to do this periodically with our finances, but rarely do we apply the same principle to personal aspects of our lives. It is only when we allow ourselves emotional space that our true feelings surface. Many people deliberately don't give themselves enough thinking time, because they are afraid of the consequences of facing the deceptions they have constructed. How often have you heard people cry, 'I don't have time!' when they are pressed to respond or make a decision. Life can't be lived successfully on automatic, and we can't indefinitely make busy-ness an excuse for not facing painful truths.

CIVILITY

Have you noticed how when you show courtesy to a fellow citizen it seems to have a knock-on effect? I've noticed this repeatedly when I've been driving. Let someone out of a side turning or give way in difficult circumstances and that motorist will often show similar consideration to someone else further down the road. (Obviously this doesn't always happen; some people are perpetually selfish and blinkered to the idea of doing strangers a good turn.) Despite the ones who don't prove the rule, I like the idea of civility snowballing and benefiting a succession of people. In many small ways we can generate a sense of well being in others and so make the world a better place.

WHAT GOES AROUND...

Civility concerns how we behave in the outside world as anonymous beings. We can cultivate a similar circle of good will through the behaviour we adopt to those with whom we have direct dealings. If we try to do our best by other people we will find we are rewarded. This is not to advise that you deliberately do something in the hope of gaining by it – there seems to be an in-built mechanism to prevent this – but it is amazing how good you feel when you behave unselfishly.

FINDING OUR DIRECTION

Sometimes unwittingly we prevent ourselves from finding our direction in life. We can be so busy dealing with the externals of life that we don't pay attention to how we feel deep down. Our interior life holds the key to our real desires. If we ignore these we can set up a conflict that can have wide-ranging negative effects. Obviously there are different ways of communicating with the inner you. Usually, though, it's when we're not thinking about anything in particular or having our minds taken over by the numerous examples of 'white noise' that surround us. Try to give yourself regular quiet times when that small, yet highly significant, voice inside can be heard. Don't try to concentrate. Just relax. You will be surprised at the thoughts that come to you.

SMILING ON LIFE

When life isn't going well, we can feel hard done by. For some reason or another, lady luck isn't on our side, and it isn't our fault. There is nothing more likely to prevent success than the belief that we are one of life's victims. All of us have good spells and bad spells. No one escapes the topsy-turvy nature of life, and very few people have all good or all bad. It may be a cliché, but we are apt to learn more from the bad spells than the good ones, because it is so easy to take what happens to us in the good spells for granted.

The artist Raoul Dufy was once asked if life had smiled on him. He responded by saying that he had 'smiled on life'. I can't think of a better reply.

SOMETHING WORTHWHILE

Unless we experience success we can't fully understand its nature, or perhaps I should say 'our' nature. The fulfilment of any goal is followed by a feeling of 'What's next?' and a search for the next challenge. Success concerned with piling up wealth can soon cease to be interesting or exciting, and the question 'What's next?' can take on a deeper meaning. Success that is not seen as being of worth by the person who has achieved it can be very unsatisfying. I once heard a very successful businessman say that he felt he had to do something worthwhile before he died. This, he said, would be the 'ultimate success'.

THE SELFISH GENE

There is scientific evidence for the notion that we are born selfish and it is our natural state (read Richard Dawkins' The Selfish Gene). This can be a very useful excuse for people who want to put their scruples aside to obtain a goal. Selfishness is not inevitable if we are to achieve our goals, and it is certainly not desirable. As the saying goes, 'No man is an island'. Think of the many ways in which you are dependent on other people and how society binds us together. If we are to contribute positively to the greater good, we must be mindful of how our actions impinge on others. If you want to achieve something that is really worthwhile, you have to try to be unselfish.

GREED

For capitalism to be successful — ie, profitable — it requires a certain degree of self-interest, not to say greed. Self-interest I can accept but not greed. It is, after all, one of the seven deadly sins. Greed says there's no such thing as too much, there's no such thing as enough. We all like to live well, but a point is reached where we don't actually need any more, whether it is food, clothes, consumer durables or other creature comforts. For someone to want to go on making money beyond this point suggests a psychological flaw. Some kinds of success can also lose their lustre quite quickly. The successes that endure feed us at a very basic level of our being and are unrelated to the desire to acquire or possess. Success does not have to be conspicuous and as with consumption it can be taken in quietly without fuss.

THE BIG I AM

I have heard top businessmen talk about making money being a lonely business, because of the necessity of taking all the big decisions by themselves and having to be secretive about their plans for fear that an indiscreet word might lead to them being scuppered. Self-reliance is essential to the success of any venture, particularly if reaching your goal seems to rely solely on your input. It can be instructive to stand back and assess your degree of aloneness. The Easyway method was my creation, but I'm not sure I could have come up with it had I not had the help and support of others. In any success there are always lucky breaks, helpers and providers who smooth the way. Never forget them or fail to appreciate their contribution.

CRISIS MANAGEMENT

We don't find out how successful we are until we have to cope with problems. These aren't the antitheses of success. Sometimes they are the prerequisites for it. It is easy to take it as a personal affront when things are difficult. But, as we have already seen, this attitude won't solve any difficulties we find ourselves in and may possibly make them worse. You might lose a loved one or have to face up to your mortality earlier than expected. Being perceived as successful in material terms won't help you to cope any better with these types of crisis than somebody who does not have your advantages. How good we are at taking life's blows on the chin will depend on the mechanisms we have developed for dealing with them. Often these mechanisms become part of our panoply of life skills without us realizing – that is, if we have lived in the right way, accepting challenges and trying to do our best.

LOSING LABELS

In the US buses are called 'loser cruisers'. I rarely use public transport these days. Like a lot of people, I prefer the convenience and comfort of my car. But it would never have occurred to me to regard people who catch buses as belonging to some sort of sub-strata of society. Labels can be very dangerous things, especially when we use them to bump ourselves up at the expense of others. To deem a person a 'loser' – ie, unsuccessful – because they use a cheap mode of transport is to use a faulty measure of worth. Defining people we don't know by such arbitrary means narrows our focus on life. The more we separate ourselves off the less connected we are to reality in its widest sense.

CREAM OR SOUR MILK?

Cream will eventually rise to the surface, as will talent. However, none of us starts off as 'cream' in the sense of being assured the success we want, and it really is down to us whether we turn into cream or sour milk. We can blame a bad start for delaying or putting paid to our chances of success, but this would be to misunderstand the true situation. What we are doesn't necessarily equate with how we were brought up. Each of us is born with an indefinable something that owes nothing to upbringing. People who have risen to the top in their chosen field against all the odds would confirm this, I'm sure. Adversity might make success more difficult to attain in some situations but it does not preclude it altogether, and in some instances it may actually provide a catalyst.

LADY LUCK

Some might believe that if you haven't got her on your side, you might as well give up. Luck's a funny thing. Sometimes what appears to be a stroke of good fortune doesn't lead to what we hoped it might, and equally misfortunes can turn out to be exactly the opposite – the 'every cloud has a silver lining' syndrome. You could be forgiven for believing that luck is some arbitrary entity that flies in and out of the window on a whim. Whichever side of the coin turns up for us depends largely on our input. Achievers make their own good fortune by attracting it to them by their efforts. Working towards a goal is a bit like creating an irresistible force that will reflect back at itself. Whether it reflects good or bad luck depends on you.

COST BENEFITS

It is usually assumed that success benefits us. If we get a rise in salary or a better job we can afford more and better things and we are more likely to be respected by people who do not know us. But what happens when the perceived advantages are no longer forthcoming and we lose the status that goes with it? Perhaps, through no fault of our own, we are made redundant or the business we are engaged in fails. We are no different as people but find ourselves in a new situation. Instead of being regarded as a success we are now perceived as a failure, one of life's losers. Material success is by its nature fickle and can't be relied upon.

CREATIVITY

To those of us who aren't artistic the performing arts can seem to provide a very potent kind of success. Imagine being an actor, musician or comic and having an audience in the palm of your hand. But, of course, such people live with that old adage, 'You're only as good as your last performance', in the backs of their minds. One night they might go down a storm and on the next their performance might fall flat. They might be able to blame the audience for being unresponsive, but not entirely. If ever there was a business to breed insecurity, show business is it. When it goes well it provides a terrific 'high' – admittedly followed by a terrific 'low' – but success is fleeting and, in some areas of the arts, often comes either side of long periods of 'resting'.

TAKING STOCK

By this stage you are probably wondering whether the words 'Easyway' and 'success' are mutually exclusive: achieving success entails a great deal of hard work over long periods with little chance of sustainability. That is indeed the case if you believe in the illusion of success. If you believe in that you will ultimately be disappointed. The illusion can't provide what you really need, which is the kind of success that is ever-present and can always be relied upon.

CONTRIBUTORS TO SUCCESS

One of the great illusions of success is that it is solely down to you whether you achieve it. Anyone who has ever achieved anything knows this to be false. Of course, you have to commit your effort and intelligence to it in the first place, but once you have set out on your path you will encounter many determiners along the route, not least the contribution other people make to your success. Never under-estimate their role or be foolish enough to think that they can be taken for granted.

THE REALITY OF SUCCESS

Notwithstanding what I have just declared, one of the great truths of success is that it is solely down to you. You are solely in charge of how you live your life, and essentially real, sustainable success derives from this. Every day of our lives as adults throws up choices. On a frivolous level at any given time we can choose what we wear and eat, whether we watch television or listen to the radio, whether we read a newspaper or a book. We can also choose whether we are pleasant to other people or grumpy or sarcastic, whether we are fair in our dealings and whether we take other people into consideration. Whichever choice we make will depend largely on how we perceive ourselves.

THROUGH A LOOKING GLASS BLINDLY

It is said that if we could only see ourselves as others do we would get an almighty shock. It might be that we don't really think about how we are in relation to others, except in terms of how we measure up superficially: has he/she got nicer clothes, a more desirable car, a better job. As for whether other people like us – this is not always an accurate yardstick. We might attract hostility from someone because we are more popular or better at something. We are not going to be liked by everyone. Sometimes people's reasons for revising their opinion of someone can be very dubious. It never ceases to amaze me how a footballer can be revered at a club one season but if he subsequently leaves and then returns to play a match against his old club it is highly likely he will be targeted with abuse. The 'fans' who behave in this way would probably argue that the footballer in question has forfeited their loyalty, but surely not their goodwill?

EXPECTING A RETURN

Too often how we perceive people depends on what we get out of them. Using the analogy of the footballer again, if he were to stay at that club until he was past his best the 'fans' would probably be howling for him to be transferred. What price loyalty then? If the footballer makes or saves goals he's wonderful, but when he doesn't he's useless. Real life can be like that when we expect a constant return from other people. If we are not careful our relationships – with family, friends and work colleagues – can be reduced to a series of one-sided contracts. Everything becomes conditional on someone else giving us what we want, and if they don't we will look elsewhere. If we get into the habit of demanding, we lose the capacity for spontaneity and natural generosity.

THE BUZZ OF DOING

It may be that as we near achieving a goal on which we have expended enormous energy and emotion, our success is not as we envisaged it would be at the outset. We are almost discontented or disappointed with what we are left with at the end. There is a brilliant song by Peggy Lee which exemplifies this —'Is this All There Is?' I'm afraid, in some instances, yes! The thing about success is that it's the doing in order to be successful that is the interesting and rewarding bit, not the being successful. Ask any person who excels in their field what they get the biggest buzz out of and they will tell you it is the 'doing'.

DOING WHAT YOU WANT TO DO

All the genuinely successful people I know are doing what they want to do and living in the way that they want to live. They are not stuck in a job they hate or with a partner they despise. One of the odd things about finding the key to success is that it forces you to address aspects of your life that you should have sorted out years before but haven't. It is so easy to divert your mind or energies instead of getting to grips with the aspects of your life that provide the least satisfaction. Just as we will try to hide traces of dirt or disharmony when someone calls round, so we tend to put the best face on our deeper dissatisfactions, with ourselves, others or situations. OK, so no one likes the whole world to know their personal business, but the very act of disguising can be an indication of our unwillingness to tackle problems. Those problems are the success spoilers.

SHEDDING ASSUMPTIONS

It's amazingly easy to gather assumptions and not realize how they can bog us down. Too often they become knee-jerk responses. It's a good idea to re-assess them and ask if they are still valid. The pattern of our lives can become similarly fixed. Are you where you want to be? If you're not, why aren't you? You may find the answers to these questions difficult to find. We are remarkably resistant to change, even when deep down we want it. The familiar is comfortable, no matter how much we might moan about it. How often do you reassess where you are and reach the conclusion that you can't do anything about it? Dismantle the barriers, don't just eye them and decide they are too high or too difficult to overcome.

INVESTING IN PEOPLE

You've probably heard of this scheme; it's when large companies try to demonstrate to the outside world that they are great employers and possess a corporate heart of gold. I've noticed that investing in people tends to go out of the window when times are tough economically. Getting in touch with your employees, concerning yourself with their career development and actually helping them to achieve it isn't appropriate when your company's got its back to the wall. I don't understand this argument. Obviously if a company's business is contracting then everyone involved should expect to tighten their belts. But a company's ethos should not change as a consequence. If the commitment to investing in people is genuine it should be able to withstand adversity and probably better than companies that are not subscribing to this principle.

INVESTING IN INTEGRITY

In western society we are taught that getting to the top is all-important. Getting to the top means being 'the best', No. 1. Interestingly it's only about being 'the best' – or successful – in a very limited sense, in one particular thing. In business it might be about making the most money; it would be nice to think it was always about making the best products or offering the best service. How often have you heard people say, in respect of business, that it's 'dog eat dog' or 'it's tough out there'? This is really shorthand for saying that anything goes. There are plenty examples of top executives, men and women, who are prepared to lie and cheat to make that last dollar. They don't need that dollar but they must have it. The word 'enough' is not in their vocabulary. Anyone who behaves like this forfeits success, because real success is based on integrity.

INVESTING IN OURSELVES

No matter how we earn our living we must always try to do the right thing. We hear stories about so-called 'whistle blowers' who try to draw attention to some wrong or misapprehension about a particular state of affairs. The case closest to my own heart is that of the US scientist working in the tobacco industry who contradicted his bosses' assertions that tobacco wasn't harmful. His research told him it was and he was not going to tell a lie. When we encounter injustice, mistreatment and downright lies, we must find the strength to oppose them. This might seem a tall order, but unless we try to be true to our principles, we will disappoint ourselves and true success will elude us.

THE EASYWAY
CLINIC LIST

AUSTRALIA
Melbourne
148 Central Road
Nunawading, 3131, Victoria
Tel/Fax: 039894 8866
Therapist: Trudy Ward
email: tw.easyway@bigpond.com

AUSTRIA
website: www.allen-carr.at

Sessions all over Austria
Free line telephone for information
and booking: 0800-Rauchen
(0800 7282436)
Sonnenring 21
A-8724 Spielberg
Tel: 03512 44755
Fax: 03512 44768
Therapist: Erich Kellermann
and Team
email: info@allen-carr.at

BELGIUM
website: www.allen-carr.be

Antwerp
Koningin Astridplein 27
B-9150 Bazel
Tel: 03 281 6255
Fax: 03 744 0608
Therapist: Dirk Nielandt
email: easyway@online.be

CANADA
Vancouver
412-2150 W. Broadway
BC V6K 4L9
Tel: 604 737 1113
Fax: 604 737 1116
Mobile: 604 785 1717
Therapist: Damian O'Hara
email: damiano@telus.net

CARIBBEAN

Antilles
11 Lot du Moulin
97190 Gosier

Guadeloupe
Tel: 05 90 84 95 21
Fax: 05 90 84 60 87
Therapist: Fabiana de Oliveira
email: allencaraibes@wanadoo.fr

COLOMBIA
Bogota
Cra. 9 No. 77-19
Tel: 313 3030 or 211 7662
Therapists: Felipe Calderon and
Jose Manuel Duran
email: positron@cc-net.net

DENMARK
website: www.easywaydk.dk

Copenhagen
Asger Rygsgade 16, 1th
1727 Copenhagen V
Tel: 03331 0476
Mobile: 5190 3536
Therapist: Mette Fonss
email: mettef@image.dk

ECUADOR

Quito
Gaspar de Villarroel E9-59y
Av. Shyris, 3er piso
Tel/Fax: 02 56 33 44
Tel: 02 82 09 20 or 02 46 94 68
Therapist: Ingrid Wittich
email: toisan@pi.pro.ec

FRANCE
website: www.allencarr.fr

Marseille
70 Rue St Ferreol, 13006
Freephone: 0800 15 57 40
Tel: 04 91 33 54 55
Fax: 04 91 33 32 77
Therapist: Erick Serre
email: info@allencarr.fr

Montpellier
1051 rue de Las Sorbes, 34070
Tel: 0467 412960
Therapist: Dominique Hertogh

Paris
125 Blvd. Montparnasse, 75006
Freephone: 0800 15 57 40
Tel: 04 91 33 54 55
Therapist: Erick Serre

Perpignan
1 Rue Pierre Curie, 66000
Tel: 04 68 34 40 68
Therapist: Eugene Salas
E-mail: eugenesalas@minitel.net

Toulouse
54 Avenue Crampel, 31400
Tel: 0800 15 57 40

GERMANY
website: www.allen-carr.de
email: info@allen-carr.de
Sessions all over Germany.
Free line telephone for
information: 0800RAUCHEN
(0800 07282436)
Central booking line: 01803
201717
Aussere Munchener Str. 34B
D-83026 Rosenheim
Tel: 08031 463067
Fax: 08031 463068
Therapists: Erich Kellermann
and Team

ICELAND
Reykjavik
Ljosheimar 4, 104
Tel: 354 553 9590
Fax: 354 588 7060
Therapists: Petur Einarsson
and Valgeir Skagfjord
email: easyway@simnet.is

IRELAND

Connaught
Tel/Fax: 094 67925
Therapist: Pat Melody Dunne
Dublin
44 Beverly Heights
Knocklyon, 16
Tel: 01 494 1644
Tel/Fax: 01 495 2757
Therapist: Brenda Sweeney
email: seansw@iol.ie

Munster
Tel/Fax: 056 54911
Therapist: Catherine Power
Hernandez
email: powerhernandez@eircom.net

ITALY

Milan
Studio Pavanello
Piazza Argentina 2, 20124
Mobile: 0348 354 7774
or 0322 980 350
Therapist: Francesca Cesati
email: fcesati@blueyonder.co.uk

NETHERLANDS
website: www.allencarr.nl
email: amsterdam@allencarr.nl

Amsterdam
Pythagorasstraat 22
1098 GC
Tel: 020 465 4665
Fax: 020 465 6682
Therapist: Eveline De Mooij
email: amsterdam@allencarr.nl

Nijmegen
Dominicanenstraat 4, 6521 KD
Tel: 024 360 33 05
Therapist: Jacqueline van den Bosch
email: nijmegen@allencarr.nl

Rotterdam
Mathenesserlaan 290
3021 HV
Tel: 010 244 07 09
Fax: 010 244 07 10
Therapist: Kitty van't Hof
email: rotterdam@allencarr.nl

Utrecht
De Beaufortlaan 22B
3768 MJ Soestduinen (gem. Soest)
Tel: 035 602 94 58
Therapist: Paula Rooduijn
email: soest@allencarr.nl

NEW ZEALAND

Auckland
Tel: 096265390
Therapist: Vickie Macrae
email: macrazies@xtra.co.nz

PORTUGAL

Oporto
Rua Fernandes Tomas
424-2° Sala 5
4000-210 Porto
Tel: 351 225 102840
Fax: 351 229 407234
Therapist: Fatima Helder
(weight clinic only)
email: easyweigh@mail.telepac.pt
www.fatimahelder.com

Rua dos Castanheiros, 97
4455-089 Lavra-Matosinhos
Tel: 229 958698
Fax: 229 955507
Therapist: Ria Monteiro
email: slofmont@mail.telepac.pt

SPAIN
website:
www.comodejardefumar.com

Madrid and Barcelona
(other areas also available)
Tel: 902 10 28 10
Fax: 942 83 25 84
Therapists: Geoffrey Molloy
and Rhea Sivi and Team
email:
easyway@comodejardefumar.com

SOUTH AFRICA

Capetown
PO Box 5269, Helderberg
Somerset West 7135
Tel: 083 600 5555
Fax: 083 8 600 5555
Therapist: Dr. Charles Nel
email easyway@allencarr.co.za